I0475650

An Honest Kindle Booksales Blueprint

How to Break Out of the No-Sales Self-Publishing Basement to Start Earning Routine and Consistent Passive Kindle Income

By **Dr. Robert C. Worstell**

Table of Contents

Bonus

Get No-Charge Access to
Writing and Publishing Materials
from Our Library Collection
Instant Access – Join Here

Click or type into your browser:

http://livesensical.com/go/writingbooks/

The Problem That Keeps Self-Publishing Authors Poor and Unknown

The average author walks onto this wild-west publishing scene clueless and ripe for picking by predators.

Most rely on hope instead of duplicating proved models.

But they don't know where to look or how to decide between all these "helpful" publishing services.

Statistically, self published authors have kept following the same patterns in all the surveys that have come out. A decade of improved opportunities hasn't enabled the vast majority of them to achieve a livable income from writing alone.

What most self-publishing authors have in common:

- Most authors make $500 a year on average.
- Most authors publish one book.
- Most books sell only 250-500 units during the author's lifetime.
- Not too surprisingly, they do no real marketing.

(See these survey links in the Appendix.)

What is keeping them that way?

Amazon is known as the self-publishing graveyard – over 3 million books available and growing by 10's of thousands of new ebooks published daily.

Most authors don't know what they are doing and rely on "hope marketing"

A rare few authors make 6-figure incomes from Amazon and peripheral sales. But their start is on Amazon Kindle, as this is the most highly-leveraged site for ebook sales. Amazon has around 70% of online sales for ebooks, which equates to a 19.5% share of all books sold internationally.

The idea to this study is that if Kindle sales can be cracked, this opens other venues for sales outside of Amazon.

Several individuals have laid out plans, programs, and "blueprints" for getting maximum possible sales from Kindle. None of these agree 100%, except in cases where they are following one of the others as mentor and are simply repeating that mentor's approach.

These systems are usually expensive to buy (and their add-on services are even more.)

Beginning authors don't know what they don't know. And have no funds for expensive marketing add-ons. As well, most of these "blueprints" may be incorrect or inefficient. But there is no way a new author will know this.

Too often, the courses become simply feeder lines for upsells to additional services. (Making money selling equipment to Gold Rush miners instead of helping them find their gold.)

That's why this research was undertaken and this book was written. All these courses and books each present a ton of data, and most of it conflicting to some degree (or completely) with other courses. This book is an effort to cut through the fog and find that trail that leads to where you want to go.

What we are all looking for:

To launch a successful book on Kindle that can be leveraged for other successful sales on Kindle and beyond. We want to generate a living, passive income from book sales.

What we need more of:

An author who knows and can use simple steps to enable any book to sell well and continue selling. Any author, any book. That's the possibility.

What we want to find out:

- The consistent factors that are used successfully in all these courses.
- The minimum requirements to succeed.

What's the best we can hope for:

Ideally , we'd have regular and ongoing sales for all new books released to Amazon Kindle.

These new books then increase earlier books in the series or by that author (rising tide.)

This basic and simple blueprint is validated, available, and easily accessed by new authors so they can build their own viable income from Kindle sales alone within a year or two. After that they can then leverage their sales to develop an independent lifestyle from writing and publishing alone.

The situation we are facing:

How to launch successfully and continue to sell in volume isn't known, proved, or made simply available to new authors and so their work doesn't sell, they give up hope, and keep their wage-slave job.

Where The Self-Published Author Begins - Way Behind the Starting Line

There are a few limiting factors in the mindset of the beginning self-publishing author:

> 1) You don't know what you don't know.

> 2) You may think you know, but these untested datums can be false.

> 3) "Burnt once, twice shy."

All these set you way back behind the real starting line. (Believe me, I've been there and done that myself.)

If you're honest with yourself, you'll graduate from the first one and start reading everything you can find about the topic. If you just read Amazon's manuals about how to publish, you'll do OK, but they don't cover how to market and get your book sold.

The other books out there can be good, but just buying bestselling books doesn't mean they'll tell you what actually works. Because many of these authors have worked out how to game the system.

Note: The cheapest way to go about finding what you need to know is to put ("[search term] filetype:pdf") into a Google search, then download and read everything you can. But cheap (or free) doesn't mean you're going to save time.

The faster way is to get a decent course to teach you a whole system. Unfortunately, most of these courses are there to sell you something else, not to just teach you what you need to know. And you have to have a source of money to invest in your education, since your book still isn't selling on Amazon worth a hoot.

These courses are also booby-trapped in one degree or another with approaches which are special to that course and its creator (their "Unique Selling Proposition") and doesn't mean it's better, just different.

These course creators have only found a single way which worked for them, and now push this route on every novice author who comes to them (and pays their price.)

The only sure way seems to be the track of this book, where you get all the courses and books on this subject and then see what they all have in common. Then you can work out the natural systems which affect all book sales and book launches. Expensive, time-consuming.

And until now, you had to invest considerable income into learning the basics through several expensive courses before you could work it out for yourself – and start making income to pay down those costs.

But here you have in your hands a book where someone else has already "gone and done it."

The point is persistence. That is the main tool you need to achieve any goal.

How to Get Everything You Want From a Book Launch (and More...)

The reasons for writing and publishing mostly boil down to a handful of reasons.

How people express these are usually this way:

> A) More income from my book sales now, and in the future. (Money)
>
> B) Improved network - more people I can pitch offers to. (List Building > Money)
>
> C) Increased reputation to promote my paid speaking gigs, or consulting, or coaching. (Celebrity > Money)
>
> D) A passion project you care deeply about and you only want to reach as many people as possible (Passion > Other Exchange)

There is a fifth one that isn't touched on by any of these courses or in their materials:

> E) Improving value to other's lives. (Open-handed Value > Other Exchange)

You'll find this last one transcends the others and is the only one which can't be booby-trapped. When you give more value, you are then contributed to in return. The more open-handed you give that value, the more it comes back to you. People want to sign up, they want your next books, they respect you, and they want to help with any project you are doing.

While the first four are completely valid, moving up to the fifth is where the best results are found. (See Maslow's Hierarchy of Motivation, particularly the last work he did on this. Link in Appendix.)

Once you know your primary motivation, then we can work it backwards from there. "Begin with the end in mind" is a phrase attributed to Socrates. Multi-millionaires like T. Harv Eker and Tony Robbins have popularized this in our own era.

(You can also use this above scale to determine what other "authorities" in this field are actually doing, and if they are there to help you, or help themselves to your pocketbook.)

You start out with the product you want to achieve, and then work out the steps you should be taking to get there. Often you won't see all the steps. Jack Canfield refers to the idea of driving a car at night, only able to see a couple hundred feet away through the headlights. But if you drive safely based on what you can see, you can get from one side of the U.S. continent to the other, just seeing a little bit ahead at a time.

I've gone down this road a bit ahead of you, so let's see what that trail looks like...

How the Big Boys Sell You Their Big Toys

I already was spoiled from the early days of bulk-uploading PLR and Public Domain material and earning enough from these to pay for my full-time research and writing. And then they changed the rules so you can't do that anymore. It helps that I also run a working farm, so have no real overhead. There's my secret to financial freedom. After you pay off your bills and learn to live within your income, you can do whatever you like.

But the next question was, "When is this 6-figure income supposed to show up?"

And what I like to do is to figure things out. Since I had nothing else scheduled, the game was afoot...

What makes a book successful in sales

The recent research has been working out how to get more sales, especially outside of Amazon. However, it came back to the point that in order to be a success out there, you have to first be a real success inside the Kindle walled garden. It was all about leveraging those sales to then build a sales record you can take to distributors who will get your book into stores and outlets who want to buy it.

If your book isn't where they are looking, then they can't buy it.

Getting the books and courses on how to succeed on Kindle apparently narrowed down to the question of how to launch a book successfully. So here we are.

These books and courses can be analyzed by what they include as well as what they leave out. One of them mentioned being able to SEO your Kindle book and just dropped the subject. This then gave me the reason to do my own research and publish what I found. (See Appendix for that research.)

That data is really part of the broader subject of how to make a reliable income online as a self-publishing writer.

Nick Stephenson reminded me that most authors rely on "hope marketing" to get their book sold. This is where an author has a single book and publishes it on Amazon as an ebook. That author will tell their friends and family about it, then just sits back and hopes it sells.

Now Nick's course is expensive and huge. It's not for beginners. But the funny thing is almost all of these courses aren't really there to honestly help beginners. Many have huge sections detailing what it takes to get your book ready for publishing. What those "intro" sections accomplish is to tell you that you ought to hire out people to do it for you - preferably someone they recommend who pays them a commission.

It's back to that same Catch-22: keep your day job to cover your expenses, which then keeps you from doing what you most love to do. Because your writing isn't paying its own way.

Most of these courses are closer to subsidy (vanity) publishing setups. Authors that know they have questions (and have money) will pay someone to help them. Author's that can't afford to pay for help will have to figure it out on their own.

Some of this is pretty well known. There are many decent and hype-free, no- or low-cost books on the basics of writing and publishing now.

Where we are starting here is where an author has already figured out how to publish (and all that data is freely available from Amazon or elsewhere online by a search.) We should be able to help any author move from published author to having a decent passive income from publishing by launching their books properly from here on out.

There is a gap in all these courses from where a person starts and where they start making decent income online. It does take work. Hard work. You'll never "get rich quick" in this universe or any other. Because humanity isn't built that way. You have to give before you can get. Cause and Effect. Oldest law known.

The list of usual suspects

Here's the well-known (and high-priced) courses I've gotten access to:

- Nick Stephenson's 10,000 Readers
- Mark Dawson's Self Publishing Formula
- Tom Morkes' Publishers' Empire
- Chandler Bolt's Self Publishing School
- Steve Scott's Authority Self-Publishing
- and several others not worth mentioning.

Each one has a nice experience overall. But all seem to have forgotten their own roots. High-priced courses aren't useful to an author who is just starting out. Of course, the best way to get the core data is to sign up for their free launch webinars or videos and save these to your own hard drive for later viewing and analysis. The good courses will give their basic principles away in those videos. If they don't give you anything useful, you have at least been entertained.

Most of these have a lot of great data on how to format your book and their own ideas of what a launch should look like. However, they all assume you already have an active list of email subscribers - because they do. Sure, they pay the idea lip service. But there are missing steps.

I've also searched around these various online programs, books, and webinars about "How to Get Your First 1,000 Fans." But they are really a bunch of junk. The weirdest advice I commonly heard was to "send out a tweet to all your followers to get them to sign up." The tragedy: that single datum was repeated by several seemingly well-meaning, but clueless "influencers." All you'd get from that would be a bunch of freebie-seeking lookie-loo's.

> *A real list is a set of buyers*
> *who want to buy your next book.*

There are those who tell you to advertise for email subscribers, but then tell you not to mix these into your regular list, as they aren't up to the point of buying from you. Meanwhile, they've told people to go ahead and spend money (their day job pays for it) to get people on a list.

The "list" is the their big item, because then you can send out email to these when you have a new release so it will get a lot of buys the first week and Amazon will then start pushing it to their other buyers.

They've got their target right, but they forgot to give that new author any arrows to shoot.

You can see the flaws in asking a new author with maybe one book self-published to then start spending money

...first for their course and maybe some upsells,

...and then for Facebook or Twitter or YouTube ads,

...and then have to convert these people over into buyers.

Meanwhile, there are "services" you can get to have it all done for you.

You're looking at huge holes in their logic. They seem like they forgot how it was when they started out. But they aren't trying to find dead-broke first-time authors. They want to find rich first time authors who have money to "invest."

Keep your day jobs, either way.

Oh, and what are you getting from these guys meanwhile? Emails with affiliate offers designed to get you to part with your money again. Endless down-spiral, like water down a drain.

There is one course - Geoff Shaw's Kindling - which escapes that mold. You can get it for about a hundred bucks with a discount coupon (see Appendix) and all the data any new author needs is available.

While all these above have private Facebook groups, I only found Shaw's to be one that I frequented regularly to get more data. Because between his course and his FB group, it's hard to say which fire-hose is easier to drink from.

Meanwhile, all of these courses claimed to be successful in creating 5- and 6-figure incomes for their graduates. We already know some have holes in them. Let's compare to find out more...

Following the Trail of Supposed Author Success

What's promoted online as author-training advice doesn't add up to reality. That shouldn't really be a surprise to any of us. None of the authors of these courses were intentionally out to deceive, it's just that they were all missing data. So their course would fail, their free books would mislead.

And again, they are meant to be income sources. One of the factors in price-setting is that if you make it pricey enough, people will take it seriously to earn their income back.

I've taken more than a few courses over the past couple of years in an attempt to sort this out for myself. (So you can say I've literally paid my dues.)

In addition to those courses, I also searched through my own years of collected of material and also searched online for all available PDFs I could find. (PDF's were chosen as these are usually the format where you'll get complete packages of data.)

Their launch data and marketing prescriptions were extracted, then the common points laid out on a spreadsheet.

And where there were controversies (strong opinions on two sides of an issue) the point was researched online to find a resolution.

While I had 11 sources to begin with, two were found to be clones of another, so were combined. This gave us 9 approaches.

In this review of author training courses, the scene turned out not too far different than what was known already.

Each of these courses would help get your book sold. Some have bona fide records of authors they helped to make a regular 5- or even 6-figure income from single book sales alone (but no record of what those authors paid to get that result.) By boiling these down and cross-comparing the courses, we have been able to actually work out the natural systems at work that you can apply.

Again, the control point is that the new author should be able to pay for any extras from current book income. Chicken-and-Egg theory applies: get the author making income somehow, some way from their existing books, and *then* they'll be able to reinvest. Only then.

Applying the natural systems to writing and publishing and selling books is no rocket science. We just have to narrow them down.

Here's a short-handed preview:

- You're going to have to write more than a single book.

- You're going to have to work at this.

- It won't happen in a month or five months. Probably a year or two is more like it, but that's is based mostly on authors who had about 10 books already written when they started trying to sell them via Amazon.

- That means you're going to have to think and act for long-term results.

- Any new author can work up to this.

There does seem to be a narrow path to follow that can lead you out of the labyrinth of false data and crush-sell marketing.

The idea here is to figure out what was essential to the new author just starting out, and what would they have to have immediately to launch their books and what would they grow into as their sales succeeded.

Next was to take all this material, put it onto a grid and see what is held in common. That's a start, anyway.

The Big Grid:

	Navid Moazzez	Johnny Pederson – Kindling	Tim Grahl	Geoff Shaw – Kindling	Lisa Cartwright & Steve Windsor	Jeff Walker (Affiliates and email)	Steve Scott, Chandler Bolt (Same, same)	Tom Morkes (Same, same)	Nick Stephenson, Mark Dawson	
Affiliates						y	y			2
Influencers: Podcasters / Book Bloggers		y					y	y		3
Series of books	y			y				y	y	3
Createspace version	y						y	y	y	4
Softlaunch							y	y	y	3
ARC's + Advance, Ambassador, Street team	y			y		y	y	y	y	6
FB Ads	y								y	2
Social media alerts	y	y				y	y	y		5
Low price during launch	y					y	y	y	y	5
Permafree				y					y	2
Wide distribution	y			y					y	3
KDP Select	y			?	y		y	y		4
Get Reviews	y		y		y		y	y	y	6
Reader magnet	y	?	y	y	y		y	y	y	7

Summary:

Reader magnets - 7

Get Reviews - 6

Use KDP Select - 4

Permafree - 2

Low price during launch - 5

Social media promotion - 5

Facebook Ads - 2

Ambassador/Street team with Advance Review Copies - 6

Soft launch - 3

Createspace version - 4

Create Series of Books - 3

Affiliates involved - 2

The Key Points:

Mailing list. If you have a mailing list, you can affect your sales. Most people mention using a **Reader Magnet** (also called various things) to get email subscribers. This is a free giveaway in exchange for opting in to an email list. Then these subscribers are invited into a select group of "Ambassadors" (also going by numerous names) who get Advance Review Copies (ARC's) of the books and are asked to leave reviews. This action usually results in immediate sales.

All these sources apparently use email subscribers if not emphasized.

KDP Select vs. Broad distribution. When KDP Select use was compared to wide distribution, it was close to a

50/50 split. There are advantages on both sides of this issue, having to do more with the length of the book published, where royalty payments are affected by KDP Unlimited pages read. A recent Author Earnings report showed that around 20% of top earners did not have their books in KDP Unlimited. For myself, I found that my books got traction outside of Amazon as much as a year before they started selling inside.

This then affects an author's choice of approach, and seems to be more of an issue if you are writing shorter works. Steve Scott by example, found his income dropped by one-third literally overnight when Unlimited was first implemented by Amazon. He was publishing shorter books at that time. However, he still maintains that staying in KDP gives him certain advantages, such as running a special on one book which then leads to other sales.

The KDP Select point also involve the strategy of setting the price at .99 for a short period of time. Some authors had become million-sellers (Locke) by using this strategy for all their books. Smashwords surveys have routinely shown that this price point doesn't give highest sales or highest royalties. (Amazon has since changed that .99 algorithm.)

Permafree. While having the first book in a series as "permafree" was disputed, the number of people giving something away for free to get email subscribers was the highest-agreed point.

Facebook Ads. The use of FB or other ads is not well supported by this survey. The and other independent ads are used by many authors, but there is no consistent mention of these. That said, Dawson's course is a very precise writeup of how to implement these.

Also, some holes in this survey showed up:

Having books in series, or at least multiple published books, was pointed out with emphasis by those who were successful in doing that. Other studies have shown that authors who were succeeding best did have a large volume of books online, that any later release would improve the sales of earlier books. Where these book were by the same author (pen name) or by series, Amazon would recommend them more.

Audio came up in two courses, but only as an afterthought to publishing both ebooks and CreateSpace paperbacks. (One was a mentor to the other.)

Jeff Walker's Product Launch Formula was compared to these to see if anything was applicable to Kindle ebook launches. Practically, his approach is based on digital products that are promoted and enabled by affiliate sales, who used email to increase sales. He has published on Amazon, but his system isn't particularly designed to work within the Amazon eco-system. (As a sidebar, several of these authors use Walker's "sideways sales letter" with a series of videos to pitch their product.)

One final point was the use of "**Influencers**" which essentially boiled down to guest blogging and podcast interviews. This is the most basic form of promotion - extending your audience by getting someone else to recommend you to theirs. (More on Influencers later.)

The most common success points are these:

> 1. Having an and building your email list, giving away your first of series or other "Reader Magnet" to get buyers subscribed.

> 2. Having a subset of these who receive Advance Review Copies and get immediate reviews and sales.

3. Having all possible other versions of the book available for sale when the ebook goes live. This makes the ebook look more valuable and also gives other purchasing options.

4. Building relationships with bloggers and podcasters to get information about your book out to their audiences.

Of course there are some lies that came out as well...

The 7 Truths and 5 Falsehoods of Kindle Sales

There are true (workable) and false (unworkable) datums pushed by these courses. Some of these may appear to be true, but just because something is repeated over and over doesn't necessarily make it so. Long studies of these have pointed up their flaws. Again, your mileage may vary, so you have to test everything I tell you here for yourself.

False, but widely spread:

A. *You have to have a decent-sized list to get started, so spend money building a lis*t so they will buy and promote your books. Not so fast. Once you create reader's magnets inside your books and on your website, your list will build naturally over time. As well, you don't hang onto people who don't open emails. Prune regularly. If you run ads, you should mainly spend to get sales, which will then bring you opt-ins. What you want on this list is people who have bought from you. Note: its not that a mailing list is necessary, but it will allow you to leverage sales and make each new book you launch an "instant bestseller" on Kindle. A smaller list of buyers will return more income than a huge list of people who won't even open emails. (There was a recent course which said to have a list of freebie-seeking reviewers who keep getting new copies only as long as they leave reviews.)

B. *Amazon reviews and high stars are necessary.* Nope. No real data supports this. Yes, there are tons of people who push this. Practically, Amazon has continual problems with sock-puppet and bought reviews, regardless of what changes they make. (Because their system is unnatural.) You want to concentrate on people who can give you reviews which are valued by the publishing industry, which is where you are headed. No one really knows how reviews affect recommendations. Only Amazon uses reviews. People don't leave reviews naturally in high volumes, and using reviews to decide on a book is very low by study. Amazon reviews aren't trusted or considered "real reviews" outside their walled garden as they are continually gamed. It's also been noted that some books sell well with *only* poor reviews, particularly where they are timely and controversial.

C. *You have to have "influencers" on board from the outset.* Networking with other authors is a smart move, but influencers are only as valuable as their list is responsive and buys books. The value of an influencer is probably how big and active their mailing list is, not their social media followings. Raise your sales and Amazon will promote (influence) for you.

D. *Amazon Kindle is everything.* Nope. It's just the start, so you can leverage what you have to bring additional routes into play. (That 80.5% market that exists just beyond Amazon - if people can make 6-figures on Kindle alone, consider what they could make elsewhere.)

E. *Social networks are vital.* Nope. Most have now shut down their organic reach in favor of selling ads, so you have a hard time even getting out to even 10% of your followers without paying to do so. Syndicate your content instead of spending time "engaging." Get real email conversations going on where you can't do in-person meets. Social Networks are basically a fad, and some recent studies have found the majority of current users are mostly looking for passive entertainment, doing very little "engagement."

True, but mostly unknown:

1. What has been missed by most of these courses is the point of continual production and publishing.

- Statistically, releasing every two weeks has the greatest effect on sales. Individual splashes don't.

- Write shorter stories at first, and then work up a model which allows a new book to be published every other week.

- First four (or eight) need to be ready at first blush.

2. The second point mostly missed is having all possible versions available at the same time. Paperback, audiobook, CD (and hardback for half- and full-collections.) These show how valuable the ebook is and also can sell better. Meanwhile, these are the page-count lengths which can get you sales outside Amazon.

3. Success route for promotion is by doing podcast and radio interviews, which have to be regular, if not daily. This is your proven influencer route. Start with smaller guest-starved shows and move to bigger ones.

4. List building occurs naturally, with early adopters and Ambassadors growing over time. Which then can be leveraged to increase sales. The more you publish, the more reader magnets are out there, the faster your list grows.

5. For non-fiction, have someone help you build a course around these books. This is additional sales and brings them to your site.

6. The general idea is to make your book sell well on Kindle, and then get other sales via paperback and audio CD sales elsewhere (via wholesalers and distributors.)

7. Your use of Amazon Kindle is as a very profitable lead magnet to build your own list and bring these to your website. You are working for Kindle, but they are also working for you. If Amazon shuts down your account tomorrow, you could survive. Think about it.

How Author Training Cabals Sell You Their Goods - And Keep You Broke

You'll also see that these author-training guys tend to run in groups, where they know and recommend each other's courses. They may or may not tell you that they are getting an affiliate payment for each sale that comes in through those "buddy connections."

These are like the "good old boy" networks which have been around since before history. The Internet Marketers are infamous for this, since they each do a new launch with a new product about twice a year. They coordinate with each other so that there are always new monthly releases.

For each release, the others send out mailings to their list and rake in commissions from those sales. Each marketer in turn gets all the buyers from the other's lists. The one with the most recent product launch has the hottest list full of the most recent buyers, and so will get the most affiliate commissions from the next launch.

They also appear on each other's podcasts and webinars to get their lists excited. They lend their "authority" to these other marketers so their list will buy those products, too.

(The discerning buyer will see that if these guys lend their credibility to some scammy marketer, that shoots their own authority in the foot.)

The people on those lists, by the way, are trained to buy the latest over and over. Meaning that they are people who can pay around $12,000 per year for books, materials, and courses. (Keep your day job.)

Statistically, only 3 percent of the students signing up will actually finish the course and 3 percent of those actually use that course to make their money back. The people in the infomercials who have made ridiculous profits are those who have probably worked out their own system and use this as a thin veneer on top. We'll never know. Oh - and that last percentage is also 3 percent. So you have a 1 in 10,000 chance of earning 6-figures by following their systems.

But these buyers have some very nice collections of materials on their shelves at home.

You are different, however. You are discerning and test everything for yourself.

You know that all true success is exceptional, so to succeed you have to be exceptional. And by reading this book, you are firmly on that path.

That path to success is only discovered by studying the successful...

6 Unknown Success Principles Every Author Uses to Succeed

In studying successful book selling-authors, there are only a few principles stand out as mostly unknown:

You only need write decent books and then market them decently to make decent income. Continue that formula to make decent passive income. We covered this earlier and it's worth repeating:

- There have always been great books which were poorly marketed and sold poorly.

- There have always been poor books which were marketed brilliantly and became bestsellers.

- You only have to write a decent book that's decently marketed to make decent income.

- Lots of decent books make even more decent income.

Bestselling authors aren't best <u>writing</u> authors, they are best <u>marketing</u> authors. Behind every book on a bestseller list is a marketing wonk. This is usually the marketer-as-author, not author-as-marketer. This also usually has a marketing team, not just an individual learning and doing it by themselves.

All promotion is getting in front of different audiences and enabling them to join your audience. This is all there is. Audio (podcasts and radio interviews) are best because they have the "theater of the mind" factor, where the listener adds background material to envision what is being described. The term "influencer" is more hype than accurate. Celebrities aren't necessarily influencers, since their followers may not buy and read books.

People who constantly hype about how many books they published - and how much money they made – are very possibly the worst person to learn from. Because they are using a very old, old tactic of claiming authority so you'll follow them blindly. A recent course I thought was really good turned out to be just a rehash of a book printed a couple of years earlier. (And his rehash added a handful of fads that just complicated the whole scene. Yes, I got a refund.) The real success is quite modest and is more concerned about *your* progress rather than their own history.

There is no one definition for "platform." Social media isn't a platform, and hasn't proved to be effective in getting sales. A blog can be part of one, you can get sales from one and guest blog for others. A podcast can be part of one, as you can sell books on one and also be interviewed by other podcasts. A mailing list is part of every successful platform I've ever studied. A network of people you can help with their success is also consistent. A platform means "how can you market this book through your own lines." Platform = Marketing. Period. Part of them are friends, part of them are fans, part of them are your personal network. The minimum platform is your mailing list and a website with your own domain. But that's not enough by itself.

Not all "influencers" are equal. Some are bums. In this day, we have celebrities who are only famous for being famous. The media follow these just as much as they follow criminals and terrorists. Because the media follows someone doesn't mean anything (except maybe to stay away from them.) The best influencers are behind the camera or microphone and don't put themselves in front of it as a subject. TV talk shows are seemingly an exception. Johnnie Carson was famous, but why? Consistently delivering the goods his audience wanted. For him, it was variety entertainment. The early TV celebrities Lawrence Welk and Ted Mack, as well as the modern America's Got Talent, the Voice, and others have this same phenomenon. Consistently delivering the goods their audience wants. This is where long-running blogs and podcasts and radio shows are where you want to start. Of course, you'll need to work up from the "small fry" to get onto the bigger ones. But that is the real scope of your marketing. You don't want celebrities, you want partners. You help their audience by giving value, and they help invite their audience to join yours.

Your book starts and ends with marketing. Period. You start the book by marketing, and conclude it by marketing. Writing is the middle of the sandwich, but you hold onto that by the two sides. The "bread" makes your sandwich able to be packaged. When it's packaged, it can be sold. You study the market you are writing the book for. You create a hook which will get readers curious. You then write the book based on that hook. Elsewhere, I've said to write your hook, title, and description before you start writing anything. If you have a book written otherwise, then you can try to fix a non-selling book by doing that marketing research now, writing the hook/title/description newly, then rereading the entire book from the viewpoint of that one person who fits the ideal reader for your book from that audience. If the book still fits, great. If you have to do some minor revising, fine. If you need to start over, then leave that book up the way it is and publish a new one. (Come back later to make it part of some series and add in a reader magnet.)

Other Myths About Amazon Publishing Exposed

Practically, most of the conventional wisdom about publishing and selling your books on Amazon is false (like most conventional wisdom elsewhere.) I bring these to you as a bonus so you can test these for yourself.

Here are some:

- *Your book need to look like a traditionally published book: size and cover, particularly.*

This applies mostly to fiction. People expect vampire novels and steampunk to have certain looks about them. Romance, for instance, usually has semi-naked bodies embracing. Thrillers do not. That's painting with a broad brush, but you get my point. I've read that the publishing size of fiction is usually smaller than 6x9. However, this means more time in special formatting and the extra expense of using a POD publisher who will produce those sizes.

The trick is, like fiction genres themselves, you need to follow conventions that buyers expect. But you want your cover to stand out compared to the others. Having a larger book might add to your advantage as the cover is more easily seen on shelves. But booksellers might not want to stock them as they take slightly more room. You need to go visit a big bookstore for yourself with a small measuring tape and see what they are actually carrying.

Non-fiction is fine for 6x9 books, although there are other sizes used. Graphic novels are much larger. Children's books are as big as regular letter size (8.5 x 11) but can be smaller and different shaped. Different shapes, special inserts, all cost money and can turn your book into a one-of-a-kind high-ticket printing nightmare you pay extra for.

Always make your presentation decisions against best reader experience.

- *You need to buy ISBN's for all your books*

There are two types of people who care about ISBN's: bookstores who hate Amazon (and won't stock CreateSpace or Amazon-published books) and snooty reviewers.

Regular readers simply don't care.

That said, having your own publishing imprint has a lot of advantages when you need to look like an independent publisher rather than a self-publishing author. Distributors would rather deal with publishing companies than a lot of individual self-publishing authors, who usually don't know what they are doing and take some hand-holding.

Ebooks don't require ISBN's, but you can track anything that has one, so this is useful when you want to find which bookstore is stocking your book, and which library has it.

A useful number you can get for free is an ISSN from the Library of Congress. This enables your title to get into WorldCat. Note that this encompasses all book-versions of that title, ebook, paperback, hardback, audiobook, etc. With your book on WorldCat, you can add in all sorts of meta data. This promotes your book to librarians, who can then buy them.

- *You need to invest in professional editing.*

The real truth is that you need to provide the best possible reader experience.

The worst (most expensive) advice along this line comes from those who sell the services. When you get an unending stream about how the quality of your book is worth they cost, it means you're probably paying for their new house or car.

Look over your book from the best possible reader experience. Proofing is usual. But doesn't have to be expensive. And a good developmental editor is also the most expensive. Writers starting out have to work from no income other than their day job. The trick in this case is to write shorter works which aren't such a pain to review and revise and proof. They are also perfect for testing a new genre. On Kindle, they are known as "short reads". Or you can move up to novella's, which are usually under 40K words (per Wikipedia.)

The sequence of self-editing is usually in three or four proofs, and the final one being sent out to another set of eyes for proof-reading, to catch typo's. But you can also swap proofs with other authors, or get a local English major to do it for some other favor. Smaller word-counts allow you to self-edit your books into shape without having to have an external editor. Shawn Coyne wrote his "Story Grid" just to train authors to do their own editing.

If the reader likes it, <u>that's</u> what counts. Learn from your Amazon reviews, but don't take them seriously. (And never, ever respond to trolls.)

The other side of the coin is someone like John Locke, who gamed Amazon's systems to become one of their first "million-seller" authors. (Kept his books at .99 and bought reviews, both of which won't give you any advantages today.) His books have some pretty scathing reviews, but they sold. So they must have something in them which readers like. And Amazon was recommending them, so they sold more books than other authors. And Amanda Hocking's first books had numerous typos in them.

You don't have to have incredible quality to sell, **you just have to have a decent reader experience** so they want to buy your *next* one.

You aren't there to become the next million-book bestseller. You're there to help entertain people with the books they are looking for.

The point to all of this is to build your own audience, the ones that like *your* style of storytelling. Be true to them.

Avoiding the Amazon JOB Trap

Earning passive income isn't just writing more books.

That idea is just a route to working for Amazon without any perks or job security.

The secrets as to why this is are already covered:

1. You need to publish in series.
2. You need to work smarter, not harder.

This is the key approach that Geoff Shaw's Kindling course revealed.

- Readers who like your book want more books by you.

- So you publish in series.

- This makes your other books show up in the Also-Boughts for every book you publish.

- When you publish every two weeks, in shorter lengths, these book sales tend to boost your earlier books in that series, keeping their sales rank higher.

Note: this was all done by publishing alone, no advertising.

That's a perfect approach for beginning authors.

You should have a minimum of three ebooks to make a series. Then adding a collection of all three at the end would make sense. Each ebook is about 8-10K words long, so if they aren't all that popular, you have only spent a month or so at this particular genre. If they are, then expand that series to 6 or 8 total. Collect them all up at the end and publish a paperback and hardback, both POD.

Authors who write single books are naïve. They stumble into Amazon's anti-scammer traps. These are also known as the 30-, 60-, and 90-day "cliffs."

This is included here as this new data came up just as this book was getting ready to publish. It came from a 2013 book by David Gaughran, called "Let's Get Visible: How To Get Noticed And Sell More Books" (See link in Appendix.)

He's the first person I've found to name the Amazon Algorithm by name.

As Gaughran describes it, Amazon had to deal with scammers who were taking advantage of getting a lot of sales and reviews on a single day and then riding out the wave of recommendations by Amazon. Meanwhile, their product sucked and the 1-star reviews started mounting up.

So Amazon created a rolling 30-day average, with emphasis on recent sales. Anything that spikes now comes back down just as fast. What Amazon rewards is books that naturally go up and stay up. Any spike in sales then means a drop later on as that peak disappears from the average.

Sales then look like they drop off a cliff. And so, the name.

The 60- and 90-day "cliffs" are due to how Amazon promotes your book internally. Specifics aren't known, but the only solution seems to be to crank out more books.

What it does penalize is the author who cranks out a 60-80K book every few months. By the time they can get it edited and proofed, their last book has been forgotten by the readers and Amazon, so they are starting over with another new release.

In other books in this series, I've discussed how you make more income from the same amount of writing by selling small parts, then collecting all of these to sell the whole. (This is reportedly the current strategy of E. L. James as she works up the next in her 50 Shades of Gray series.) What this does is to give you a working income while you write, instead of simply going from feast to famine and back.

More importantly, the reading public doesn't forget you. Publishing every two weeks is doable for most authors. You have another book which can be sold that carries on where the last left off. (Writing in a serial format is even better – see my book on this particular subject. Link in Appendix.)

Yes, you've probably figured out that is why I put all these books into a series, even though they've been stretched out over 3 years. (Starting to smarten up in my later days...)

For a profitable launch strategy, these are the points:

> a. Publish short reads every two weeks.

> b. Publish in a series in the same genre/category.

> c. Collect up your series at intervals and sell these as well.

> d. If you do promote during your launch, spread out the dates they hit, so they cover at least two weeks, if not a month.

Added Note: Surveys by Smashwords' Coker and Author Earnings have pointed out that the very long books have sold better. In their 2015 study, AE supposed that this might be because they were collections. This seems to finally be that explanation. Collect up your earlier books that cost $3.99 each and sell a bunch of them for $5.99 or more. Obvious value.

But you can see the fallacy of trying to write a 300K word book over a year and then taking another 6 months to a year to get it edited and published, only to have a reader go through it in a month and ask you for the next, please. Meanwhile, the price point has to be below $9.99 to get any decent royalties.

And from that single month of your launch, you need to make enough to cover your expenses for the next year and a half.

Writing shorter lengths and publishing more frequently *in a series* tends to solve reader wants and authors needs.

Theoretically publishing some 48 books a year at $2.99, with 12 collections of four at $3.99, 6 collections of 8 at $4.99, and a final mega-collection at $6.99 or higher – what does that come to? 67 books in a year, each selling longer than your single book that dropped to obscurity after its first 30 days.

The naive author, feverishly writing single books and publishing every 90 days is only getting four books out per year, with the collection being available just in time for Christmas (where it's competing with all the Big 5 releases.)

The smart author writes in series, starts a new series when they have enough of the earlier ones, compiles collections regularly, publishes every two weeks, and has steady income through the *whole* year. (And they publish their big collections in January or August, by the way, where peak sales might just get them on renown bestseller lists.)

Smart authors quit their day job when they start making decent enough money to never have to look back.

Naive authors start working for Amazon.

(Amazon is a decent enough publishing partner, but pays no benefits to freelance authors, let alone a living wage. If you want to work for Amazon, find out when they are hiring and sign a contract, put on a uniform.)

Me? I'd rather write, publish, and cherish my independence.

A Working Guide to Publishing Your Passive Income Empire, Step-By-Step.

Of course, and as always, test everything I say and prove it for yourself. It isn't worth anything unless you can use it for yourself.

Strategy:

0. We start out with short reads (5k - 8K words) to test the market and improve your writing skills.

I. Phase One:

Start publishing in sets of four, posted two weeks apart for optimal effect.

- First one is permafree.

- 2nd and rest at $2.99 (for non-fiction)

- Collection of four at $4.99 or $5.99

Ia. Paperback, audio, and CD are published simultaneously for each ebook. Published slightly ahead of that ebook. Minimum on CreateSpace is 28 pages.

1b. At 2K words per day, creating a book one week and then editing and creating a cover and meta-data for it the next will probably wind up leapfrogging your books so that your launch subscriber list has time to review it before you publish. Write well ahead of publishing as much as you want, so that you can publish a minimum of three books in a series, plus that collection.

Notes:

- Reader Magnet opt-in's front and back, which then build your list.

- FB ads can be profitably run on the collection to boost sales.

- Sales boost opt-ins to list.

- In theory, you could keep up a regular production of content published every two weeks.

- This planning is set up to expand starting from no books and a small list, if any.

II. Expansion of Influence

- Start getting book blogger reviews and radio/podcast interviews on a regular basis.

- Seasons are set up in hardcopy versions to go into libraries as paperback and hardback. They just need a data block for libraries and accepted into wholesalers.

- List grows larger and Ambassador sub-list is built, in addition to Early notifiers.

III. Building Team to expand promotion

- Daily radio and podcast shows.

- Idea: Target east coast with stacked advertising to get into bestseller NYT and other lists and ramp sales outside of Amazon.

The Program:

0. Get into the Kindling course to understand the steps below. (Link in Appendix)

1. Set up a site that allows you to have landing pages. Start a blog or podcast.

2. Create some giveaways to start getting email subscribers.

3. Do your homework on genre/category, keywords, targeted audience demographics. Concentrate an a specific genre and produce a series of content for this exact area.

4. Create a series of four short books as part of a series:

- Find a hook for the series and each book - 20 words
- Write a paragraph for each book - elevator speech
- Create title, description, cover for those books
- Plot and write each book.
- Self-edit into shape. Get them proofed.

5. If you have any people on your email list, get them to review them.

6. Port to Kindle two weeks apart

- 1st is perma-free - port to D2D to make the others free, then get Amazon to price-match.
- Reader magnet is initially for some other cheatsheet or content upgrade.
- 2nd and rest are 2.99 – same reader magnet as above
- Then publish collection for 4.99.
- Revise lead magnet later as needed.

7. Publish paperbacks of each book and collection before the ebook goes live, through CS.

8. Audio is created as part of editing and is posted on podcast, aligned with your Kindle schedule, linking to each individual book and collection

- Also built up as audiobook and distributed through Author's Republic.

9. All books are sold on your own site through their individual sales pages. Your list gets early notification and post release discounts.

10. Port ebooks to HummingbirdDM, OverDrive and e-Sentral for wider ebook distribution.

11. Get Global Distribution on Lulu to get your hardcopy books into Ingram. Ensure you get your own ISBN for that version and is tied to your own imprint so wholesalers will accept them more easily and get them into libraries for you. (It's mainly a problem with Createspace-owned ISBNs, as well as other Amazon imprints.)

How to Re-Market an Under-performing Self-Published Book

0. Open up your Ambassador list to all comers - email existing subscribers.

1. Collect up (or write) a set of books to go along with this one to make a series.

1a. Select one of the books as perma-free and

- Do steps 2-6 below on it,

- Publish everywhere possible at $0,

- Get Amazon to match price on this.

Do these next steps a week or two apart, so you can see if they help or depress sales:

2. Verify their hook, category, keywords, title/subtitle, description, and editorial reviews.

3. Verify the cover

4. Revise the copy as needed

- To include a proper reader magnet. And create that reader magnet if you don't have one or need a better one.

- To make all the chapter headings media-genic so they could each be the subject of a radio talk show by itself. Each chapter should make a captivating tweet.

- To ensure there are hooks at every chapter start and cliff-hangers/enticing previews at its end.

- If non-fiction, give short bullet summaries of useful steps outlined in that chapter they can start to use right now.

5. Proof that new copy.

6. Send out that new copy to your Ambassador team for their feedback. Nudge them up on it if they don't open the email.

7. Set the price higher than normal. 8.99 probably.

8. Schedule it for re-launch two weeks after you send it out.

9. Day of launch:

- Get analytics on that book and start checking this daily. Take screenshots with time and date.

- Drop price to .99 and announce this to Ambassadors.

- Publish the book to all other ebook sales outlets possible through D2D (preferably) or Lulu at normal price.

10. Three days later (or so) announce the low price to your entire list and tell them they have four days to get it at this price.

11. Send out an email a day before you increase the price, then increase it to normal price (3.99 or higher) when you do.

12. Of course, you're still watching daily analytics on this to see and record the effects.

13. Watch it for the next two weeks.

14. Repeat steps 2-13 for the next book in the series. Rinse/repeat for entire series. (New books written for the series obviously don't need all these steps.)

15. Set up a collection on Kindle that has half or all of these books in it.

16. Meanwhile, arrange to record all the books to audio, preferably while you have it out for proofing.

- Post this audio as podcast - edit the book as you can to include links to podcast within that chapter in the book, and full set of links in the back. Ensure podcast is promoted in the book as part of the Look Inside.

- Publish the audio book through Author's Republic

- Publish the spoken word album through CD-Baby

17. Publish paperback version (paperback) through CreateSpace.

18. Publish hardback (and another paperback) through Lulu with Global Distribution to get sales through Ingram as well.

19. Update your own site's sales page to include all discounts and let your list know they are there.

An Outline of the Non-Advertising Route to Book Publishing Success

This is one route I can say I've been there and done that. Since ebooks had their breakthrough in 2009 or so, I've done my share in testing these waters.

A recent roundup shows I've published a few hundred titles in various formats. None were promoted other than a new cover and description.

And this has given me my financial freedom. But like cheesecake and scenic vistas, you can never have enough.

Expensive advertising and promotion is recommended by celebrity authors (and those who want you to pay them to pitch your book.) This isn't necessary at all.

Recent research shows that *a longish period of consistent marketing is what makes books get onto and stay on the bestseller lists*. And for authors, that means getting interviewed regularly, in addition to anything else you are doing (such as public appearances.) Getting interviewed by media just means learning how to give them what they know their audience wants. That means doing a little homework instead of getting a second job to pay for ongoing ads.

Most of the conventional wisdom about promoting books includes live TV and radio shots, as well as book tours. This isn't necessarily true. Factually, physical book tours are a inefficient at best and at worst, a waste of your time and money. You can do radio and podcast interviews from your home. You can also do guest posts on various blogs from there.

Some people like getting on TV. I don't. It would take a full day of travel just to get to a megalopolis of either coast from my rural Midwestern farm. As well, having to be cooped up with all sorts of people, smells, and other inconveniences. Long TSA lines. No wide-open spaces and fresh air or farm-fresh, home-cooked meals for days on that junket.

Around the same time I found that datum, I also found another - that authors who publish accurately and in series can let their books (and Amazon) do all their promotion. These authors can move into 6-figures simply, and with not that many books. Some do it within a year of starting to write and publish in earnest. No ads.

This doesn't mean you can't and shouldn't contact the various book blog reviewers and submit your book. The trick is to work smart and keep track of which ones worked.

Sticking to Amazon ebook publishing alone does tend to keep you inside the Kindle walled garden. By itself it doesn't give you a diversified income from writing. The authors studied here all created additional versions of their books which gave them income independent of their Kindle books.

(You can and should invest that "excess" 6-figure income to further diversify, but that is way outside what we cover here.)

To expand your sales into that 80.5% of books sold outside Kindle, the trick seems to be in contacting libraries and indie bookstores to get them to stock your books. Meanwhile, part of your pitch to them is the promotion you are doing to their patrons. Perhaps that means by then you can afford to run regular promotion to their area for that series of books. But that library and indie bookstore promotion itself is just emails and maybe some calls.

Meanwhile, there are wholesalers such as OverDrive and e-Sentral which will carry your ebooks for only time investment of uploading your titles in their format.)

Lulu.com will get your hardcopies into Ingram with no cost to you, other than proofing an actual copy of your book.

If you want bestseller status, you have to figure what you want it for and is that worth the trade-off. What cost are you willing to pay?

All I'm saying here is that it can be done simply, and only with the excess profits from your books. You just have to get them earning income first, and build on that.

Running your book publishing as a business seems the only route out. The authors who are taking the amateur approach to their writing and publishing never make an income, because they don't work at it. There is no 6-figure income which is based on set-and-forget that I've found.

This book started with the too-common case of the one-book amateur author making next to zero sales. Now we know why and what to do about it.

How much you want out of your writing and publishing is up to you.

Your life is your choice. As always.

The Final Chapter Always Tells the Future Story Starting

My time on this subject is nearly done. You've gotten my best research for a few years now and this book actually wraps everything up that I can see from here.

All that's left now is some very intensive testing.

My research was always "how does this stuff work?" And this book concluded the last of the pure research needed for any self-publishing author to find out what they need to know in order to set up a real independent publishing scene and diversify their income streams to be independent of Amazon's walled garden.

Fiction authors graduate to having all versions of their book/idea-containers take the stage in their own right. Maybe even films (DVD's) eventually. There is no limit to your abilities or your vision.

Non-fiction authors can create courses and memberships and also get into speaking engagements, coaching, consulting, and so on. (Of course Fiction authors make incredible speakers, too...)

I saw today in an mastermind group that there is still a vital need for these books and courses on how to create and publish books. I've told you the both the good and great courses you can invest in. But you should work to stick within your budget and then use the "excess" income to pay down your debts. You can get financially free with just that method.

If you use what is in these relatively inexpensive books in this series you'll have more than what you actually need to get started. *The caveat is to test everything for yourself.*

The industry is in constant change and shifts are happening all the time.

You can become a published author with a steady income that gives you any amount of financial freedom - all you can stand.

I believe in you.

Your next steps could give you permanent financial freedom.

The door is now open

Here's the rough layout of how to pry the Amazon walled garden door open so you can come and go as you want:

1. Amazon Kindle is so well known that it's simple to leverage it and get an operating base.

2. Meanwhile, you've learned to publish on all other ebook outlets and in all possible book versions.

3. You set up your indie publishing imprint with your own ISBN's. And start getting reviews from people who are respected in the wide world outside Amazon publishing.

4. Your paperbacks and hardbacks get into wholesalers and have their own record from selling on Amazon (as they have ISBN's which can be tracked by Nielsen.)

5. Start getting them into libraries and indie bookstores.

6. The podcasting you've been doing with your audio books is a start. You expand this onto radio and podcast interviews as a regular daily/weekly action. (This is how Robert Kiyosaki of "Rich Dad, Poor Dad" as well as Jack Canfield of "Chicken Soup for the Soul" both got started.)

7. You can then invest heavily in East Coast promotion to get onto various publications "bestseller lists" while you meanwhile also get distributors to get your books into all

other possible outlets. Bestseller lists can further accelerate your booksales, if done right.

8. You've been building your marketing and production team so now you can either go back to writing, or do whatever it is that you like most. Enjoy life to its fullest.

Where I got all this data is laid out in the Appendix. You should have all you need there, if you test everything for yourself.

I'm between steps 2 and 3 myself right now, but this is the online business I'm building. Those are my steps to take. They seem logical and workable.

You have your own path to travel.

If you want to follow this journey, just click on the links in the front or back of this book. I'll keep you updated as part of my mailing list, for sure. Your company is welcome, as well as your help.

See you up the line.

Appendix

Bibliography

Other books in this series

Visit http://livesensical.com/book-series/publishing-and-writing/

Available on Amazon, Lulu, and as Pay What You Want

Really Simple Writing & Publishing

Learn How to Write, Design, Format, Upload, and Sell Your Own Book for Low Cost or Free.

J'APE: Just Another Publicity Excuse

How to Publish Your (Kindle) Book for Shameless Self-Promotion and Profit

Publish. Profit. Independence.

How to Earn Extra Income and Financial Freedom by Publishing on Your Own

How to Write Less and Profit More

A Rich Adventure in Short Read Kindle Publishing - http://amzn.com/B01AQPPQM0

Writing Serial Fiction in the Real World

A Simple, Tongue-in-Cheek Guide to Writing and Publishing Episodic eBooks for Profit on Amazon (and Elsewhere.)

How to Help Librarians Fall in Love With Your Self-Published Book

...and Get More Sales When They Do.

Cracking the Kindle Sales Code

How to Search Engine Optimize Your Titles and Descriptions so Amazon Promotes Your Book and Recommends Buyers to You at No Cost

An Honest Kindle Booksales Blueprint

How to Break Out of the No-Sales Amazon Self-Publishing Basement and Start Routinely Earning Regular Passive Income From Your Kindle Booksales Without Added Expense or Tricks

Links

A Key Book

"Let's Get Visible: How To Get Noticed And Sell More Books" by David Gaughran http://amzn.com/B00CPQ6YYI

Courses (not affiliate links)

- Nick Stephenson's 10,000 Readers (http://noorosha.com/10k-readers)
- Mark Dawson's Self Publishing Formula (http://selfpublishingformula.com/)
- Tom Morkes' Publishers' Empire (http://tommorkes.com/empire/)
- Chandler Bolt's Self Publishing School (http://self-publishingschool.com/)
- Steve Scott's Authority Self-Publishing (http://authority.pub/apa-waitlist/)

- Geoff Shaw's Kindling (use "KDSPY" for $27 discount - http://www.5minutepublishing.com/kindling/)

A Failed Launch Survivor Story: I Lost $6,500 on My Last Book Launch: Details, final tally, lessons learned (https://goo.gl/FhNbmc)

PDF's (no opt-in's requred):

Tim Grahl: http://timgrahl.com/lp-book-launch-blueprint

Steven Windsor and Lise Cartwright: http://digitalfreedom.academy/freebies/Steve_Windsor_Lise_Cartwright_15-Day-Book-Launch-Blueprint.pdf

Chandler Bolt: http://onemillionactsofeducation.com/wp-content/uploads/2015/12/BookLaunch_ebook.pdf

Jeff Walker Launch Blueprint: http://plf4.s3.amazonaws.com/product.launch.blueprint-v4.pdf

Joanna Penn – Author 2.0 Blueprint: http://s3.amazonaws.com/Author2zero/Author20Blueprint_010215.pdf

Surveys of Authors and Their Earnings

Here's where you can cross-check the data about average earnings from the various studies.

The overall view is that you can either get volunteer data, or rely on Author Earnings data scrapes. In general, the results are pretty similar:

> 1. Authors who have no clue what they are doing need to keep their day jobs.

 2. The successful are always exceptions.

The point of this report is to aggregate data to enable people to become that exceptional success.

http://authorearnings.com/report/may-2015-author-earnings-report/

May 2015 - No breakdown per author, just per category. Traditional (trad) authors lost 20% income due to 17% increase of pricing by Big 5 publishers, which created a 17% loss of sales.

http://authorearnings.com/report/february-2016-author-earnings-report/

Feb 2016 - Overall ebook sales have increased.

Trad publisher share of the sales units has decreased to 25%, while they still take over 47% of the income.

As far as author earnings, indie authors take home close to half of the earnings, while trad publishers get less than 25% of this pie.

Amazon is selling over a million paid downloads per day (1,064,000)

http://www.digitalbookworld.com/2015/investigating-author-publisher-dynamics-results-from-the-2015-author-survey/

2015:

2,545 authors completed the Digital Book World and Writer's Digest Survey, and 1,879 of the respondents were published authors.

10% earning $100,000 or more and 4% earning $250,000.

Most authors in the latest sample aren't making much money, and most books still sell very few copies.

About 15% make above $40K per year.

http://www.digitalbookworld.com/2013/self-publishing-debate-part3/

2013:

"Not surprisingly, most aspiring authors in the sample reported no annual income from their writing. About 19% of self-published authors in the sample also reported no annual income from their writing, compared to 6% of traditionally published authors and only 3% of hybrid authors. While most of the survey respondents clustered at the lower end of the income distribution, some authors did report earning $200,000 or more from their writing, the highest income choice on the survey: less than one percent (0.6%) of self-published authors, 4.5% of traditionally published authors, and 6.7% of hybrid authors who reported on their income. (In the chart, I have collapsed the top categories to $100,000 or more for better visibility. These aggregated category represents 1.8% of self-published authors, 8.8% of traditionally published authors, and 13.2% of hybrid authors.)

"Self-published authors in the sample earned a median income in the range of $1 to $4,999, while traditionally published authors had a median writing income of $5,000 to $9,999, and hybrid authors earned a median income of $15,000 to $19,999. Comparing authors with the same number of manuscripts (analysis not shown), there is a strong similarity in income between hybrid and traditional authors, but hybrid authors outperformed their self-published counterparts on earnings.

"Together, what these patterns suggest is that few authors are getting rich off of their writing or even earning enough from their writing to quit their day jobs. As the data for this study come from a non-scientific sample, readers are cautioned in generalizing to the entire author community; the survey responses may not be representative. At the same time, the overall pattern of findings is consistent with other studies that show that few books or few authors or even few artists of any type for that matter actually "make it" and are successful (however one defines the term). The new lesson from this study is that the chances of having a financially viable writing career may be best for hybrid authors and traditionally published authors."

http://brendahiatt.com/show-me-the-money/indie-earnings/

2014;

"This year I received responses from a total of 227 authors, representing 2,594 indie titles of which 1928 were frontlist indie titles and 666 were backlist (trad-pubbed, now indie) titles, assuming no duplicates (see above).

"AVERAGE indie earnings reported per author: $91,337

"Average number of indie-only (frontlist) titles per author: 8.45
Average number of backlist (but now indie) titles: 2.93
Average TOTAL indie titles per author: 11.43 (again, this number could be slightly inflated by any duplicate reporting)

"Perhaps slightly more useful, since averages can be skewed by outliers:
MEDIAN earnings per author: $20,000 (half of earnings fell above, half below this amount)
Earnings reported ranged from a low of $4 (which might possibly have been a typo) to a high of $2.1 million.
This works out to an AVERAGE of $7,996 per title for 2014 earnings. (If there are duplicates in the frontlist & backlist columns, average per-title earnings would be greater.)"

https://claudenougat.wordpress.com/2016/02/07/only-40-self-published-authors-are-a-success-says-amazon/

2016;

"...finally we know exactly how many self-published authors make it big: 40.

"Yes, that's not a typo.

"40 self-published authors "make money", all the others, and they number in the hundreds of thousands, don't. This interesting statistic, recently revealed in a New York Times article, applies to the Kindle Store, but since Amazon is in fact the largest digital publishing platform in the world, it is a safe bet that self-published authors are not doing any better elsewhere.

" 'Making money' here means selling more than one million e-book copies in the last five years."

http://www.publishersweekly.com/pw/by-topic/industry-news/publisher-news/article/68008-new-guild-survey-reveals-majority-of-authors-earn-below-poverty-line.html

2015:

"The survey, conducted this spring by the Codex Group, is based on responses from 1,674 Guild members, 1,406 of whom identified either as a full-time author, or a part-time one. The majority of respondents also lean older—89% are over the age of 50—and toward the traditionally published end (64%).

"So what does that Federal Poverty Level statistic mean? Given that a single person earning less than $11,670 annually sits below the poverty line, 56% of respondents would qualify, if they relied solely on income from their writing. The survey also indicated that not only are many authors earning little, they are, since 2009, also earning less. Overall, the median writing-related income among respondents dropped from $10,500 in 2009 to $8,000 2014 in 2014, a decline of 24%. The decline came for both full-time and part-time authors with full-time authors reporting a 30% drop in income to $17,500 and part-time authors seeing a 38% decrease, to $4,500."

http://publishingperspectives.com/2014/01/how-much-do-writers-earn-less-than-you-think/#.V-qcA9GglZ4

2014:

"The Guardian's Alison Flood reported on a publishing industry deeply divided. In the same week, she noted, that writer of erotica Sylvia Day signed a startling eight figure two book deal with St Martin's Press, a survey revealed that 54% of 'traditionally-published' authors (and nearly 80% of self-published authors) earn less than $1,000 a year.

"The survey of more than 9,000 writers in the 2014 Digital Book World and Writer's Digest Author Survey, was presented at last week's Digital Book World Conference. Respondents were divided into four categories: 'aspiring, self-published only, traditionally-published only, and hybrid' (meaning both self and traditionally published). Of those who filled in the survey, more than 65% described themselves as aspiring authors; 18% as self-published, 8% as traditionally published, with 6% saying that they were "pursuing hybrid careers."

"According to the survey, 'Just over 77% of self-published writers make $1,000 a year...with a startlingly high 53.9% of traditionally-published authors, and 43.6% of hybrid authors, reporting their earnings are below the same threshold. Only 0.7% of self-published writers, 1.3% of traditionally published writers, and 5.7% of hybrid writers reported earning more than $100,000 a year from their writing. (The typical writer in the sample was 'a commercial fiction writer who might also write non-fiction and who had a project in the works that might soon be ready to publish.')"

Disclaimer:

The author and publisher of this Ebook and the accompanying materials have used their best efforts in preparing this Ebook. The author and publisher make no representation or warranties with respect to the accuracy, applicability, fitness, or completeness of the contents of this Ebook. The information contained in this Ebook is strictly for educational purposes. Therefore, if you wish to apply ideas contained in this Ebook, you are taking full responsibility for your actions.

There is no implied or stated guarantee of any income or sales using the material in this book. You earn your own income through your own efforts, or lack of them.

The author and publisher disclaim any warranties (express or implied), merchantability, or fitness for any particular purpose. The author and publisher shall in no event be held liable to any party for any direct, indirect, punitive, special, incidental or other consequential damages arising directly or indirectly from any use of this material, which is provided "as is", and without warranties.

As always, the advice of a competent legal, tax, accounting or other professional should be sought. The author and publisher do not warrant the performance, effectiveness or applicability of any sites listed or linked to in this Ebook. All links are for information purposes only and are not warranted for content, accuracy or any other implied or explicit purpose.

Lawyers are funny: Your mileage may vary. "Caution Contents May Be Hot." Snowflakes get triggered; life is that way.

Index